When Life is Over

Rick Jones

CHICK
PUBLICATIONS

For a complete list of international
distributors who carry this book,
call Chick Publications or visit
www.chick.com/distrib.asp

All Scriptures are from the Authorized
King James Version of the Bible

© 2000 by Rick Jones
CHICK PUBLICATIONS
P. O. Box 3500, Ontario, Calif. 91761-1019 USA
Tel: (909) 987-0771
Fax: (909) 941-8128
Web: www.chick.com
E-mail: postmaster@chick.com
Printed in the United States of America

Fourth Printing

ISBN: 0-758903-92-8
Library of Congress Control Number: 00-092502

You *will* live forever.

The question is… *where?*

After reading this short book, you will know the truth about what awaits you after death. You will also have learned the answer to many of life's most-often-asked questions, like:

- Is there a God?
- Is there a devil?
- Is there a heaven?
- Is there a hell?
- Can I believe the Bible?
- Would a loving God really send people to hell?
- Can I know I'll go to heaven when I die?
- Aren't there many paths to heaven?
- Aren't all people the children of God?
- What makes Jesus Christ so special?
- What about all the Christians who are hypocrites?
- Isn't Christianity just for the weak?

As you will see, this book contains many Scriptures from the Bible. That's because there is no authority in the words of man, but there is ultimate authority in the words of God. As you are about to learn, the Bible is a book you can trust, and a book containing answers to life's most important questions.

Introduction

"I'll be home in twenty minutes, honey... and I've got a surprise for you."

Jessica couldn't wait. Her husband, Charles, was returning from a two week business trip.

"I'm at the airport. I have my bags and I'm heading out to the car. I can't wait to see you. I love you."

Jessica felt much better. She always worried when Charles was in the air. But with his feet safely on the ground, she breathed a sigh of relief.

Jessica waited anxiously by the front door. Every time a car passed by, she brushed back the curtains and peered out. But each time, disappointment followed. After thirty minutes, she began to pace nervously.

"Where is he?" she wondered.

"He should have been here by now."

After nearly an hour, a car door slammed in the driveway. Jessica excitedly jumped to her feet and yanked open the door, expecting to see her husband's smiling face and outstretched arms. Instead, she beheld two solemn-faced police officers. Jessica froze.

"Are you Jessica Robinson?" one officer asked.

"Yes," she quivered. "Why?... what's wrong?"

"I'm afraid we have some bad news."

Jessica began to panic.

"May we please come in?"

"Is it Charles? Is something wrong with Charles?"

"We are very sorry, Mrs. Robinson, but your husband is dead. He was hit by a drunk driver three miles from here."

Jessica shrieked in disbelief. "That's impossible! I just talked to him! We have two children to raise. We have plans... we..."

But it was true. Charles was gone. Just like that. One minute he was on the phone... the next he was dead.

Although nobody likes to think about it, someday each of us will die. Have you ever lain in bed at night, staring at the ceiling, and wondered what will happen after you breathe your last breath? Have you ever asked yourself, "Is there a God?... Is there an afterlife, or does the grave end it all?... Can I know what will happen to me?

The truth is, you *can* know the answer to each of these questions. In fact, by the time you finish reading this book, you will... ***guaranteed!***

So sit back, get comfortable, and learn how you will spend eternity. Remember, there's no guarantee you'll be alive tomorrow to read this short book, so please read it right now.

This may shock you, but the answer to every question just raised is not only available, but may have been right in your home for years. Where? Right in the Bible.

Hold on. Before you dismiss this book as a dusty, outdated relic, keep reading. The Bible is an amazing book packed with practical, real-life answers to today's toughest questions.

Don't be deceived. The Bible is not just a book written by men, it is the inspired Word of God:

*All scripture is given **by inspiration of God,** and is profitable for doctrine, for reproof, for correction, for instruction in righteousness: 2 Timothy 3:16*

Yes, men wrote down the words, but the words came directly from God:

*For the prophecy came not in old time by the will of man: but holy men of God spake **as they were moved by the Holy Ghost.** 2 Peter 1:21*

Because the Bible is so important, God promised to preserve His Word forever:

*The words of the LORD are pure words... Thou shalt keep them, O LORD, **thou shalt preserve them from this generation for ever.** Psalm 12:6-7*

Before diving into your questions about eternity, we

must first show the Bible to be a reliable source. If you are to trust this book on eternal matters, you must first be convinced it is reputable in other areas.

The Bible is a miraculous book

The Bible was written over a period of sixteen hundred years by more than forty different authors, starting around 1500 B.C. Despite the astronomical odds, all their stories mesh flawlessly because, in truth, the Bible has only one Author... God:

> *Thy word is true from the beginning: and every one of thy righteous judgments endureth for ever.*
>
> *Psalm 119:160*

Throughout history, many unbelieving scholars have studied the Bible, determined to disprove it. Instead, its miraculous accuracy often led them to become Christians instead.

Does the Bible contain fulfilled prophecies?

A major proof of the Bible's divine origin is its many fulfilled prophecies, with more coming to pass every day. No other religious book contains fulfilled prophecies.

The Bible makes at least sixty predictions regarding the Lord Jesus Christ alone. God's Word declares He would be born of a virgin (Isaiah 7:14) in Bethlehem (Micah 5:2). He would be rejected by His own people (Isaiah 53:3), and His side would be pierced (Zechariah 12:10). All these prophecies, made long before they were fulfilled, occurred exactly as the Bible foretold.

The Bible made the following prediction over seven hundred years before Christ was born:

*For unto us a child is born, unto us a son is given:
and the government shall be upon his shoulder:
and his name shall be called Wonderful,
Counsellor, The mighty God, The everlasting
Father, The Prince of Peace. Isaiah 9:6*

One of the greatest prophecies ever made concerned the crucifixion of Jesus Christ. Psalm 22:14-18 provides a descriptive and detailed account of Christ's death on the cross. Amazingly, this was written 1,000 years before the event occurred, and at that time, crucifixion had not yet even been invented.

During His earthly ministry, Jesus declared that Jerusalem would be completely destroyed (Matthew 24:2). Within a few years, it was.

Over 1,400 years before Christ was born, the Bible predicted that Israel would be regathered as a nation (Deuteronomy 30:3). In 1948, over three thousand years later, it miraculously happened. No wonder the Bible says:

*Till heaven and earth pass, one jot or one tittle
shall in no wise pass from the law, till all be fulfilled. Matthew 5:18*

My friend, the more you learn about fulfilled Bible prophecies, the more convinced you will be that this is God's holy inspired Word, and the more confidence you will have in it when planning your eternal destiny.

Is the Bible scientifically accurate?

Although the Bible is not a scientific book, its pages contain many scientific facts. Often, men took centuries to discover what the Bible had declared long ago.

In 1615, William Harvey made what many considered a brilliant discovery... that the life of all flesh is in the blood. But three thousand years earlier, the Bible declared, *"...the life of the flesh is in the blood..." (Leviticus 17:11).*

In 1475, Copernicus discovered that the earth was round and hung in space. Yet, two thousand years prior, the Bible proclaimed, *"It is he that sitteth upon the **circle of the earth"** (Isaiah 40:22).* The Bible also says of God, *"He... hangeth the earth **upon nothing"** (Job 26:7).*

In the 1840's, when Lord Rosse built what was then the world's largest telescope, man learned about the great empty space in the north. But long before, the Bible announced, *"He stretcheth out the north over **the empty place..."** (Job 26:7).*

Though the Bible is not a science book, it is one hundred percent scientifically accurate.

Is the Bible factually accurate?

You have undoubtedly heard people mock famous Bible stories. None has been more laughed at than the account of Jonah being swallowed by a great fish.

Consider this. In the December, 1992 issue of *National Geographic* magazine, University of Maryland marine biologist Eugenie Clark, who has studied whale sharks extensively, confirms in detail nearly every aspect of the Jonah story. Professor Clark writes:

> "The whale shark's unusual digestive anatomy lends itself to Jonah stories. It is easy to imagine yourself being inadvertently sucked into a whale shark's mouth..."

The Jonah story concludes when the great fish "vomited out Jonah…" (Jonah 2:10). Professor Clark:

> "Sharks have a nonviolent way of getting rid of large objects of dubious digestibility they swallow accidentally. In a process known as gastric eversion, a shark can slowly empty its cardiac stomach by turning it inside out and pushing it through the mouth."

In his book, *Explore the Book,* J. Sidlow Baxter tells about a whaling ship near the Falkland Islands in February, 1891. In attempts to harpoon a large sperm whale, one of two small boats was capsized. One man was drowned and another, James Bartley, disappeared. The whale was eventually killed and dragged on board. Sailors worked all day and into the night removing the blubber. The next day, the sailors were startled by signs of life. They cut open the fish and inside found James Bartley, doubled up and unconscious. He was revived with a bath of sea water, and within three weeks had resumed his normal duties.

The flood and Noah's ark

For years, "experts" laughed at those who believed in Noah's ark and a world-wide flood. The smart ones aren't laughing anymore. In 1959, a Turkish army captain was examining aerial photos of his country when he spotted a boat-shaped form about five hundred feet long (the same size as the Biblical ark) in the area where the Bible says Noah's ark came to rest. Many expeditions have reached the site and considerable evidence has convinced countless eye witnesses that this is in fact Noah's ark.

You see, no matter how unlikely a Bible story may appear, if God's Word says it's true, then it's true.

"Sanctify them through thy truth: **thy word is truth."** *John 17:17*

Is the Bible archeologically accurate?

Since the Bible refers to hundreds of ancient cities, kings, etc., excavations at these sites would have to reveal hard evidence, or we could easily discount the Bible as mere fable. Not to worry. So many Bible cities, names and events have been unearthed through archeology that the Bible is considered the single most important historical document in existence. In fact, many lost cities have been discovered using the Bible as a roadmap.

Here's an example. The Bible makes over forty references to the great Hittite Empire. But one hundred years ago, there was no archeological evidence to prove it ever existed. "Just another Bible myth," skeptics claimed. But in 1906, Hugo Winckler uncovered a library of 10,000 clay tablets which fully documented the lost Hittite Empire. The Bible was right all along.

Hundreds of examples could be given, but the fact is, archeological discoveries constantly confirm what the Bible declared long ago, and not one archaeological discovery has ever proven any Biblical reference to be untrue. That's because the Bible is 100% archeologically accurate.

Is the Bible historically accurate?

Many scholars recognize the Bible's amazing historic accuracy. Did you know the birth, life and death of Jesus Christ are all established historical facts? A Jewish historian (not a follower of Christ) recorded the following words around A.D. 93:

> "Now there was about this time Jesus, a wise man, if it be lawful to call him a man; for he was a doer of wonderful works... He drew over to him both many of the Jews and many of the Gentiles. He was [the] Christ. And when Pilate, at the suggestion of the principal men amongst us, had condemned him to the cross, those that loved him at the first did not forsake him; for he appeared to them alive again the third day; as the divine prophets had foretold..."[1]

You can trust the Bible in eternal matters because it is unchallenged in its historical accuracy.

Why hasn't the Bible faded away?

Many claim the Bible is an outdated book not relevant for today, yet the truth is, it's more popular than ever. It is a constant best seller, and every culture on earth has felt its influence. It has been translated into about 4,000 different languages, with more being added regularly. Why? Because God promised that:

*Heaven and earth shall pass away, but **my words shall not pass away.** Matthew 24:35*

As you read the Bible verses in this book, you can believe and trust them because they are God's words, from God's supernatural Book. Now let's begin answering some important questions.

---

1 Antiquities of the Jews, from The Life and Works of Flavius Josephus, Published by The John C. Winston Company, Pg. 535

Is there a God?

There certainly is. The Bible's very first words are "In the beginning God created the heaven and the earth" (Genesis 1:1). God doesn't attempt to prove His existence, He merely states it as an established fact.

Is there a God? Step outside some evening and gaze into the star-filled sky. Consider the billions of stars, millions of miles away. Consider the other planets, other galaxies. The Bible reminds us:

> *"The heavens declare the glory of God; and the firmament sheweth his handywork." Psalm 19:1*

Is there a God? Consider the human body. Psalm 139:14 declares we are "fearfully and wonderfully made." Let's examine one small part of the body, the human eye. Because of its extreme complexity, scientists still don't fully understand how it works. Guess who said:

> "To suppose that the eye, with all its inimitable contrivances for adjusting the focus to different distances, for admitting different amounts of light, and for the correction of spherical and chromatic aberration, could have been formed by natural selection, seems, I freely confess, absurd in the highest possible degree... The belief that an organ as perfect as the eye could have formed by natural selection is more than enough to stagger anyone."[1]

Who declared this remarkable truth? None other than the famous evolutionist, Charles Darwin. Even he recognized

1 Shute, E., *Flaws in the Theory of Evolution,* Craig Press, Nutley, NJ, 1961, pp.127-128.

that an organ as intricate and magnificent as the eye required a Creator.

Sir Isaac Newton said, "This most elegant system of suns and planets can only arise from the purpose of an intelligent and mighty Being."

Albert Einstein declared, "The harmony of natural law reveals an intelligence of such superiority that compared with it, all the systematic thinking of human beings is utterly insignificant."

Yes, there is a God. The evidence is overwhelming. And someday, we will stand before Him:

> *So then every one of us shall give account of him-self to God. Romans 14:12*

Will you be ready? By the time you finish this book, your answer can be yes.

Is there a Devil?

Just as surely as there is a God, there is also a devil. Ezekiel 28 tells us much about this evil character. He was created by God (v. 13) and lived in heaven (v. 13). God set him up as an anointed cherub (v. 14). He was perfect in beauty (v. 12), which led him to become proud (v. 17). He rebelled against God (v. 15-16), and was evicted from heaven (v. 16). Originally called Lucifer, he was banished to earth (v. 18), where he became known as Satan:

> *How art thou fallen from heaven, O Lucifer, son of the morning! how art thou cut down to the ground, which didst weaken the nations! Isaiah 14:12*

> *And the great dragon was cast out, that old ser-pent, called the Devil, and Satan, which deceiveth*

the whole world: he was cast out into the earth, and
his angels were cast out with him. Revelation 12:9

Satan is now the god of this world (2 Corinthians 4:4)
but someday he will be cast into the flames of hell (Isaiah
14:15), where he will burn for all eternity:

And the devil that deceived them was cast into the
lake of fire and brimstone, where the beast and the
false prophet are, and shall be tormented day and
night for ever and ever. Revelation 20:10

Today, he roams the earth as your unseen spiritual
enemy, working to deceive and destroy you:

Be sober, be vigilant; because your adversary the
devil, as a roaring lion, walketh about, seeking
whom he may devour: 1 Peter 5:8

Satan's ultimate goal is to see you thrown into the lake
of fire. Right now, he is furious that you are reading this
book. He hates the wonderful truths you are learning.
Please don't let him stop you from finishing this book.

Is there a Heaven?

God's holy Word assures us repeatedly that a real place
of eternal beauty and splendor called heaven does exist:

"...for God is in heaven..." Ecclesiastes 5:2

Do not I fill heaven and earth? saith the Lord?
Jeremiah 23:24

Heaven's streets are paved with gold (Revelation 21:21),
and there, nothing ever wears out (Matthew 6:20). Those
who reach this place of everlasting peace and joy will
share it with angels (Matthew 18:10) and receive eternal

rewards (Matthew 5:12). Best of all, God wants us to live there forever. Jesus said:

In my Father's house are many mansions: if it were not so, I would have told you. I go to prepare a place for you. And if I go and prepare a place for you, I will come again, and receive you unto myself; that where I am, there ye may be also.

John 14:2-3

Many skeptics claim heaven doesn't exist, but their disbelief does not change reality. During a blizzard one frigid December night, a Minnesota farmer was watching the TV news. When he saw sunbathers basking in 85 degree Hawaiian sunshine, he snickered to his wife, "I don't believe a place that beautiful really exists." Well, Hawaii does exist, whether he believes it or not. So does heaven.

Is there a Hell?

Just as surely as there is a place of eternal bliss called heaven, there is a place of everlasting punishment called hell. It's not a popular subject, but you must be aware of it. The Bible tells us about a man who went there:

And it came to pass, that the beggar died, and was carried by the angels into Abraham's bosom: the rich man also died, and was buried; And in hell he lift up his eyes, being in torments, and seeth Abraham afar off, and Lazarus in his bosom. And he cried and said, Father Abraham, have mercy on me, and send Lazarus, that he may dip the tip of his finger in water, and cool my tongue; for I am tormented in this flame. Luke 16:22-24

Our minds cannot comprehend a place this ghastly. Hell is described as an "everlasting fire" (Matthew 25:41), "eternal fire" (Jude 7), and "a furnace of fire" (Matthew 13:42). Revelation 20:10 refers to it as "the lake of fire and brimstone." Those who are doomed there "shall be tormented with fire and brimstone" (Revelation 14:10).

It is a place of "outer darkness" (Matthew 8:12) and "blackness and darkness" (Jude 13), where inhabitants endure "chains of darkness" (2 Peter 2:4) in a "bottomless pit" (Revelation 20:3).

Hell's inhabitants experience "weeping and gnashing (grinding) of teeth" (Matthew 8:12), "everlasting destruction" (2 Thessalonians 1:9), and "...the smoke of their torment ascendeth up for ever and ever" (Revelation 14:11). Worst of all, hell's population increases every day, yet it is never full (Proverbs 27:20).

This gruesome place of eternal torment was prepared for the devil and his angels (Matthew 25:41). Satan knows he will eventually be condemned there (Isaiah 14:15, Revelation 20:10). So will all those who reject God's one and only method for reaching heaven (2 Thessalonians 1:8).

Comprehending the never-ending pain of hell is impossible. To get a tiny glimpse, imagine laying your hand on a red-hot stove burner. Though your hand would only touch the flame for a fraction of a second, you would scream out in agony. Now imagine being unable to remove your hand. Even worse, picture your whole body inside the burner, with no way to escape... forever.

Though our finite minds cannot grasp the dreadfulness of hell, it's undoubtedly a destination you want to avoid.

Thanks to God's mercy, you can. You'll learn how shortly.

Would a loving God really send people to hell?

According to God's infallible Word, yes. This frequently asked question implies that God is somehow unfair because many people end up in hell. He is not. The truth is, God does not arbitrarily send people to hell. They *choose* to go there. And nobody is more heartbroken over this than God:

> *The Lord is not... willing that any should perish, but that all should come to repentance. 2 Peter 3:9*

God loves you and does not want you in hell:

> *As I live, saith the Lord God, I have no pleasure in the death of the wicked... Ezekiel 33:11*

Because God loves us so much, He paid the ultimate price to spare us from hell. He sent His only Son, Jesus Christ, to die a torturous death on the cross so we could escape hell's flames.

However, in His perfect love, God also gives us a free will. We can accept or reject His escape hatch from hell. If we reject it and burn, it is our fault, not God's.

Imagine an inmate sitting on death row. He is about to be executed when the warden appears at his cell with an official pardon signed by the governor. All this condemned man must do is accept the pardon and he can waltz out of prison a free man. But suppose he rejects the pardon and is executed. Is it the governor's fault? No. He did everything he could, but his offer was rejected.

Our eternal destiny is the same. We can accept God's offer, or we can reject it and suffer the consequences. The choice is ours. What could be more fair? Soon, you will have an opportunity to choose heaven as your eternal home. If you stop reading and do nothing, hell is where you will go.

Can I know I'll go to heaven when I die?

Let's allow God's Word to answer this question:

*"These things have I written unto you that believe on the name of the Son of God; **that ye may know that ye have eternal life...**" 1 John 5:13*

Consider this. Knowing there is a heaven and a hell, would a God who loves you want you to spend your whole life terrified of ending up in hell? Of course not. Refusing to let you know where you are headed after death would be torture of the cruelest kind.

Imagine this hypothetical scenario. A woman visits her doctor after experiencing severe stomach pain. After running several tests, he phones her and says, "I know you and your husband are leaving on a three week vacation tomorrow. I have the test results in my hand and I know what your problem is, but I'm not going to tell you until you return. But I will tell you this: it's either a minor illness, or it's a terminal disease which will cause you to die a slow, agonizing death.

Would this woman enjoy her vacation? No way! She would be tormented day and night. She would be consumed with learning her fate. Granted, this illustration is a stretch, but you get the point. For God to write in His Word that some people will burn forever in hell, but refuse to tell us how to avoid those flames would be unbelievably cruel. That's why God's Word says we can have:

*...an inheritance incorruptible, and undefiled, and that fadeth not away, **reserved in heaven for you,***
1 Peter 1:4

Want to get your reservation in? Keep reading.

Aren't there many paths to heaven, like spokes on a wheel?

Although this widespread belief sounds very poetic, it simply isn't Biblical. According to God's Word, there is only one way to heaven. Jesus preached:

*"I am the way, the truth, and the life: no man cometh unto the Father, **but by me.**" John 14:6*

Referring to Jesus, the Bible declares:

*Neither is there salvation in **any other:** for there is none other name under heaven given among men, whereby we must be saved. Acts 4:12*

Jesus says salvation is through Him alone:

***I am the door:** by me if any man enter in, he shall be saved... John 10:9*

If there were many ways to heaven, then most people would be going there. Look at the shocking words Jesus spoke to the multitudes during His sermon on the mount:

*Enter ye in at the strait gate: for wide is the gate, and broad is the way, that leadeth to destruction, and **many** there be which go in thereat: Because strait is the gate, and narrow is the way, which leadeth unto life, and **few** there be that find it.*
Matthew 7:13-14

Notice. *Many* go to destruction. *Few* find eternal life. You can be one of the few. It's up to you.

Will I make it to heaven if I do the best I can?

Millions hope to earn heaven by doing their best. But the Bible says our best will never be good enough:

> *But we are all as an unclean thing, and all our righteousnesses **are as filthy rags**... Isaiah 64:6*

Solomon, the wise man, declares:

> *For there is **not** a just man upon earth, that doeth good, and sinneth not. Ecclesiastes 7:20*

The Apostle Paul, who penned much of the New Testament, said of himself:

> *For I know that in me (that is, in my flesh,) dwelleth **no good thing**... Romans 7:18*

This same Paul said:

> *As it is written, There is **none righteous, no, not one:** Romans 3:10*

The Bible says good works will never get anybody into heaven:

> *Therefore by the deeds of the law there shall no flesh be justified in his sight... Romans 3:20*

If you believe doing your best will get you to heaven, you will be sorely disappointed.

Won't being sincerely religious get me to heaven?

God's Word says millions of well-meaning religious people will burn in hell. Jesus Himself tells us that religious people will stand before Him at judgment, thinking they'll get into heaven because of their good works:

*Many will say to me in that day, Lord, Lord, have
we not prophesied in thy name? and in thy name
have cast out devils? and in thy name done many
wonderful works? Matthew 7:22*

Can you picture these people? They preached in Jesus'
name. They cast out devils in His name. They did wonderful works in His name. So they are shocked to learn they
are being rejected from heaven. They cry out in despera-
tion, "But Lord, my religion promised me I would get in.
They told me my good works would help."

Instead Jesus will look into their eyes and proclaim:

*I never knew you: depart from me, ye that work
iniquity. Matthew 7:22-23*

Religious friend, please be warned. According to Jesus
Christ, religious people will be sent to hell. Please don't be
deceived by a religion. When Jesus walked the earth, He
hated religion. His strongest opposition came from religious people. He called the religious leaders "hypocrites,"
and "blind guides." He said they were "full of extortion
and excess" and "full of dead men's bones, and of all
uncleanness." They were "full of hypocrisy and iniquity"
and were "the children of them which killed the prophets."
Jesus called them "serpents" and a "generation of vipers"
(Matthew 23:23-33). After his scathing condemnation,
Jesus asked these religious leaders:

...how can ye escape the damnation of hell?
Matthew 23:33

Did you catch that? These sincere religious leaders were
on their way to hell. Many people are sincere, but it takes
more than sincerity to reach heaven. You must be sincerely

right. Tragically, millions of religious people are sincerely wrong.

One night, a nurse gave the wrong medication to a young hospital patient. Before her error could be detected, the patient died. Was the problem a lack of sincerity? No. The patient died because the nurse was wrong, though she sincerely wanted to help him.

In his letter to the Romans, the Apostle Paul said this of well-meaning religious people:

Brethren, my heart's desire and prayer to God for Israel is that they might be saved. For I bear them record that they have a zeal for God, but not according to knowledge. Romans 10:1-2

They were religious, and very sincere, but they were lost.

Millions of men and women will go to hell because they obeyed a religion. If you are trusting a religion to get you into heaven, beware. Jesus says it won't.

Won't I go to heaven if I'm a good person?

This sounds logical, doesn't it? From childhood, we are taught, "those who do good get rewarded, while those who do bad get punished." But being good will *never* get you to heaven. First, according to the Bible, there are no "good people:"

*They are all gone out of the way, they are together become unprofitable; **there is none that doeth good, no, not one.** Romans 3:12*

By your standards, you may consider yourself a pretty good person. But by God's standards, you fall far short. When Jesus was being crucified, two criminals hung on crosses beside Him, one on each side. Before He died, Jesus promised one of them, *"Today shalt thou be with me in paradise (Luke 23:43).*

Wait a minute! This guy had committed a crime worthy of the death penalty. Yet Jesus assured him he would go to heaven. Obviously, it wasn't because he was a good man. Shortly, you'll learn why he made it, and how you can too.

Will I go to heaven if I do what feels right in my heart?

The worst mistake you can make is doing what feels right in your heart. Millions have missed heaven for this reason. Heed God's warning, *"He that trusteth in his own heart is a fool..." (Proverbs 28:26).* Here's more insight:

The heart is deceitful above all things, and desperately wicked: who can know it? Jeremiah 17:9

When making eternal decisions, ignore what you feel in your heart. It will deceive you every time. Instead, believe the only reliable source, God's Holy Bible.

Aren't all people children of God?

This widespread misconception is never found in the Bible. All people are the *creation* of God, but only a few are the *children* of God. While conversing with a group of Jews, Jesus infuriated them by proclaiming:

*Ye are of **your father the devil,** and the lusts of your father ye will do. John 8:44*

While speaking to a sorcerer, the Apostle Paul said:

*O full of all subtility and all mischief, thou **child of the devil**... Acts 13:10*

We are all born as children of the devil, and if you have not done what it takes to become a child of God, then you remain Satan's child. But you can choose to be born into God's family today.

Okay, so how do I get to heaven?

We've examined many methods that will *not* get you to heaven. Now let's discover the one method that will get you through the pearly gates. The main problem is sin, and to understand it, we must start at the beginning.

Adam and Eve were created by God as perfect, sinless creatures. But one day, Satan, in the form of a serpent, tempted Eve to sin. She did. Soon after, Adam sinned too. As you will see, this caused a deadly sin nature to be passed down to everyone ever born.

Why is sin so dangerous?

First, sin always leads to misery, heartache and death:

...sin, when it is finished, bringeth forth death.

James 1:15

Notice the words "when it is finished." Many people mistakenly believe they have gotten away with sin because they have not yet felt its consequences. The fact is, sin just isn't finished with them yet. God's Word declares, "the wages of sin is death" (Romans 6:23), and God's Word is always right. In the end, *nobody* gets away with sin.

Sin is also dangerous because it separates us from God. Because of sin, Adam and Eve were driven out of God's presence, and because of sin, most people are separated from God's presence in heaven for eternity:

But your iniquities have separated between you and your God, and your sins have hid his face from you, that he will not hear. Isaiah 59:2

Worst of all, because of sin, Jesus Christ suffered and died on the cross:

Christ died for our sins according to the scriptures; 1 Corinthians 15:3

How important is the sin issue? If the CEO of General Motors flies from New York to Tokyo to personally handle a matter, you know it is *very* important. So how important is an issue that requires God Almighty to leave the perfection of heaven, be born on earth as a baby, then grow up and die a barbaric death on a cross? ***VERY important!***

Adam and Eve's sin caused two results. First, they were driven out of the Garden of Eden. God still loved them but would not allow sin to remain in His presence. Secondly, their sin was passed down to every person ever born:

*Wherefore, as by one man (Adam) sin entered into the world, and death by sin; and **so death passed upon all men,** for that all have sinned: Romans 5:12*

Because of their sin, everyone is born a sinner:

*For **all have sinned,** and come short of the glory of God; Romans 3:23*

*But the scripture hath concluded **all under sin...** Galatians 3:22*

Even if you only sinned once (which no one has), you would still be a sinner:

For whosoever shall keep the whole law, and yet offend in one point, he is guilty of all. James 2:10

You may be thinking, "If we are all sinners and God will never allow sin into His presence, then nobody will ever get into heaven." This leads us to the only way sin can ever be forgiven... blood:

What's so important about blood?

Throughout history, God has ordained that blood would always play a key role in the forgiveness of sins:

> *And almost all things are by the law purged with blood; and **without shedding of blood is no remission.** Hebrews 9:22*

> *...it is **the blood** that maketh an atonement for the soul. Leviticus 17:11*

Until Adam and Eve sinned, they both were naked. After their sin, God shed the blood of an innocent animal to make a covering for their now sinful bodies:

> *Unto Adam also and to his wife did the LORD God make coats of skins, and clothed them. Genesis 3:21*

This is the first recorded instance of God shedding blood to cover people's sins. Notice, Adam and Eve sinned only once, but one sin was enough to make them sinners. Thus, blood had to be shed for their sin.

What did Old Testament people do about their sins?

Throughout Old Testament times, sins were temporarily covered by the shed blood of innocent sacrificial animals. (See Leviticus 4.) But the Bible says these ongoing animal sacrifices could not permanently take away sins:

> *"...it is not possible that the blood of bulls and of goats should take away sins." Hebrews 10:4*

The Day of Atonement

Here is a beautiful picture of the role blood played in the covering of sins. God instructed the high priest to enter the holy of holies in the tabernacle once each year. But first, the high priest was required to shed the blood of an innocent animal for a sin offering.

Within the holy of holies was a box called the ark. Inside the ark lay the two tables of stone upon which God wrote the Ten Commandments. The ark was covered by a lid called the mercy seat. Every year on the day of atonement, God appeared in a cloud on the mercy seat. But before He appeared, the high priest sprinkled the blood of the sacrifice on top of the mercy seat. Thus, when God looked down, He didn't see His law inside the ark. He saw the blood on the mercy seat. You will understand the significance of this shortly.

Again, it wasn't how good or bad the people had been. They had all sinned, therefore they all needed to have their sins covered, and there was only one way... by the blood.

The Passover

Remember the passover story? The children of Israel were in bondage in Egypt, and Pharaoh refused to let them go. After several plagues, God was about to kill the first-born in every home. To protect the Hebrew children, Moses was ordered to have his people get a lamb. But not just any lamb:

Your lamb shall be without blemish... Exodus 12:5

In a moment you'll see why this was so important.

They were instructed to kill the lamb and spread it's

blood on the doorposts (Exodus 12:7). Then, when God passed through the land killing the firstborn, those with blood on the doorposts would be spared:

> *And the blood shall be to you for a token upon the houses where ye are: and **when I see the blood, I will pass over you,** and the plague shall not be upon you to destroy you, when I smite the land of Egypt. Exodus 12:13*

An innocent lamb died so people could live. Again, it didn't matter how good or bad the people were. They had all sinned, so they all required blood on their doorposts.

How did Jesus settle the sin problem?

Eventually, God revealed His plan for dealing with the sin problem once and for all. One day, a preacher known as John the Baptist made one of the most important statements ever uttered by human tongue. When he saw Jesus approaching, he announced:

> *...Behold the **Lamb of God,** which **taketh away** the sin of the world. John 1:29*

Notice two critically important parts of this statement. First, John referred to Jesus Christ as the "Lamb of God." Rather than continuing to shed the blood of sacrificial lambs, Jesus Christ had come to earth to shed His own blood as the ultimate sacrificial lamb.

Secondly, Jesus came to "take away" sin once and for all, not to cover it for a period of time:

> *As far as the east is from the west, so far hath he (Jesus) removed our transgressions (sins) from us.*
> *Psalm 103:12*

Jesus didn't die to temporarily cover our sins, He shed His blood *"for the remission of sins" (Matthew 26:28).*

What makes Jesus Christ so special?

At least four important facts about Jesus Christ must be understood. First, He always was and always will be God. Jesus Himself declared, "I and my Father are one" (John 10:30). The gospel of John opens with the words, "In the beginning was the Word (Jesus Christ), and the Word was with God, and *the Word was God* (John 1:1). When a man named Philip asked Jesus to show him the Father, Jesus replied, "...he that hath seen me hath seen the Father... (John 14:9). Paul wrote to Timothy about Jesus, saying, "God was manifest in the flesh... (1 Timothy 3:16). The Bible states, "For there are three that bear record in heaven, the Father, the Word (Jesus Christ), and the Holy Ghost: and these three are one (1 John 5:7).

Secondly, as God, Jesus Christ was sinless:

> *For he hath made him (Jesus) to be sin for us, who knew no sin... 2 Corinthians 5:21*

Since Jesus was born of a virgin, God, not Joseph, was His Father. God's pure, sinless blood flowed through the Lord's veins. That's why He was the only sacrifice that could permanently take away our sins. Remember how Old Testament law required sacrificial lambs to be without spot or blemish? They were a foreshadowing of the perfect sacrifice (Jesus) who would come to take away the sins of the entire world.

Third, Jesus is important to you and me because He willingly died to pay the price for our sins. Jesus declared:

I lay down my life, that I might take it again. No man taketh it from me, but I lay it down of myself.
                                    John 10:17-18

Jesus was not taken against His will. Nor was He powerless to escape. Jesus said:

Thinkest thou that I cannot now pray to my Father, and he shall presently give me more than twelve legions of angels? Matthew 26:53

Lastly, Jesus is special because He rose from the dead:

*And declared to be the Son of God with power, according to the spirit of holiness, **by the resurrection from the dead.** Romans 1:4*

No other religious leader in history has ever risen from the dead. Muhammad, Buddha, Joseph Smith and all others are still in their graves.

God's ultimate plan

Obviously, the sacrificing of animals could not go on forever. So, to settle the sin issue once and for all, God the Father sent God the Son (Jesus Christ) to be born on earth.

After living thirty-three sin-free years on this planet, Jesus Christ was crucified on a cross. Since Jesus never sinned, He was not required to die. So when He shed His blood, it was not for His own sins, but for the sins of all mankind. Jesus was the final sacrifice for sin forever:

So Christ was once offered to bear the sins of many... Hebrews 9:28

*But God commendeth (showed) his love toward us, in that, while we were yet sinners, **Christ died for us.** Romans 5:8*

This true story beautifully illustrates Christ's death for us:

"During the Civil War a man by the name of George Wyatt was drawn by lot to go to the front. He had a wife and six children. A young man named Richard Pratt offered to go in his stead. He was accepted and joined the ranks, bearing the name and number of George Wyatt. Before long Pratt was killed in action. The authorities later sought again to draft George Wyatt into service. He protested, entering the plea that he had died in the person of Pratt. He insisted that the authorities consult their own records as to the fact of his having died in identification with Pratt, his substitute."[1]

As sinners, we deserve to die and suffer in hell. But because Jesus Christ, our substitute, died in our place, we can be freed from the penalty of our sins and receive God's gift of eternal life.

The Bible tells us Jesus tasted death *for us*:

...that he (Jesus) by the grace of God should **taste death for every man.** *Hebrews 2:9*

What Old Testament lambs could never do, Jesus did through His death:

Neither by the blood of goats and calves, but by his own blood he entered in once into the holy place, having obtained eternal redemption for us.

Hebrews 9:12

The high priest offered animals as a temporary sacrifice for sins, but Jesus Christ (God in the flesh) offered Himself

1 L. E. Maxwell, *Born Crucified,* Moody Press, 1945, pg. 13.

as a living sacrifice to purchase our redemption by paying the full price for every sin ever committed:

> *But this man (Jesus), after he had offered* **one sac-rifice for sins for ever,** *sat down on the right hand of God; Hebrews 10:12*

> *...but now once in the end of the world hath he (Jesus) appeared to put away sin by the* **sacrifice of himself.** *Hebrews 9:26*

The high priest's work was a picture of the work Christ would do on the cross:

> *Who needeth not daily, as those high priests, to offer up sacrifice, first for his own sins, and then for the people's: for this he (Jesus) did once, when he offered up himself. Hebrews 7:27*

Remember how on the day of atonement the high priest covered the mercy seat with blood so God would see the blood instead of the law? This was another picture of what Christ would do for us. Today, when God looks down at those who have trusted His Son, Jesus Christ, He doesn't see their sins, He sees the blood of His Son.

It's not how good or bad you've been. The question is, "Have your sins been paid for by the blood of Jesus Christ?"

The Passover was another foreshadowing of the work Christ would do on the cross:

> *For even Christ our passover is sacrificed for us:*
>   *1 Corinthians 5:7*

Only Jesus, the sinless Lamb of God, could redeem us from our sins:

*Much more then, being now **justified by his blood,**
we shall be saved from wrath **through him.***
Romans 5:9

Paul stressed this point in his letter to the Colossians:

*In whom we have redemption **through his blood,**
even the forgiveness of sins... Colossians 1:14*

As the sacrificial Old Testament lamb was "without blemish," (Leviticus 9:2), so was Jesus:

*...ye were not redeemed with corruptible things, as
silver and gold... But with the precious blood of
Christ, as of a lamb **without blemish** and without
spot: 1 Peter 1:18-19*

The Apostle Paul describes Christ's death this way:

*Christ hath redeemed us from the curse of the law,
being made a curse for us... Galatians 3:13*

Never again would blood have to be shed for sins. Never again would good works have to be done to earn forgiveness. All the work was done. That's why, while hanging on the cross, Jesus cried out the words, *"**It is finished...**"* (John 19:30).

The plan of salvation was complete. What an incredible thought! God in the flesh had taken upon Himself all the sins of the world. Do you see why being "good" can't save you? As sinners, we all need a Savior, and Jesus is the only Savior:

*Look unto me, and be ye saved, all the ends of the
earth: for I am God, and **there is none else.***
Isaiah 45:22

Jesus came to earth for one reason... to die for us:

For the Son of man is come to seek and to save that which was lost. Luke 19:10

Does everyone need Jesus?

Yes. Jesus is the only hope, and the only way to heaven:

For as in Adam all die, even so in Christ shall all be made alive. 1 Corinthians 15:22

When you truly understand this, you will readily accept God's love gift. Imagine yourself on a sinking ship in freezing, shark-infested ocean waters. As the hours pass, hope fades. Then, in the distance, you spot an approaching boat. The vessel eventually arrives and a sailor throws you a line. Would he have to beg you to grab the line? Of course not, for without it you would surely die.

My friend, without Jesus as your Savior, you are lost and drifting in a sea of sin. No one can help you but Him. He alone can throw you a life-line of eternal life. Will you grasp it, and be pulled to safety, or will you push it away and drown in your sin?

A video showed two speeding race cars slam into each other. The first car crashed into a wall and burst into flames. Rescue crews rushed to the driver's aid, but could not douse the flames. The driver could not free himself from the wreckage because of the many safety belts and harnesses. Raging flames prevented rescue workers from getting close to the car. He was trapped, engulfed in flames, with no way out. Then one brave soul dove head first into the flames, quickly released the belts and freed the panicked driver.

This, too, pictures your condition. You are trapped in

your sins and the fiery flames of hell await. Without Jesus, there is no escape. But thank God, Jesus is willing and able to rescue you... if you will let Him.

Lastly, picture yourself dying of a rare disease. You have exhausted every avenue, but still you are dying. Then you hear of a doctor with a revolutionary new cure. Every patient he has treated has been completely healed. Your choices... receive the doctor's treatment and live, or refuse his help and die. The choice is simple.

Without Christ, you are facing certain eternal damnation in the lake of fire. You may have tried several religions, but never been spiritually healed. That's because religion kills, and only Doctor Jesus can heal you spiritually. And He has never lost a patient.

Please understand, this book was not written to beg you to become a Christian. Its purpose is to show you your lost condition. Look at God's warning:

And whosoever was not found written in the book of life was cast into the lake of fire. Revelation 20:15

Once you truly understand your state, you will beg Jesus to save you. You won't want to risk living another second without Him.

I'm ready. What do I have to do?

First, you must recognize and admit you are a sinner who needs a Savior. Next you must be willing to repent of your sins:

...except ye repent, ye shall all likewise perish.
Luke 13:5

Webster's Dictionary says repent means "to be sorry...

to turn from sin... to feel regret... to change one's mind."

Repentance is not doing good works. Rather, it is a heart-felt sorrow for past sins and a desire to have God change your life.

Next, you must understand that salvation comes, not through good works, but through believing in Jesus Christ and putting your complete trust in the work He finished on the cross. In a conversation with a religious man named Nicodemus, the Lord Jesus Christ declared, "whosoever **believeth in him** (Jesus) should not perish, but have eternal life (John 3:15). One verse later, Jesus said:

*"For God so loved the world, that he gave his only begotten Son, that whosoever **believeth in him** should not perish, but have everlasting life." John 3:16*

For emphasis, the Lord quickly repeats this same truth:

*"He that **believeth on him** (Jesus) is not con-demned: but he that believeth not is condemned already, because he hath not believed in the name of the only begotten Son of God." John 3:18*

John the Baptist also declared:

*He that **believeth on the Son** hath everlasting life: and he that believeth not the Son shall not see life; but the wrath of God abideth on him. John 3:36*

Jesus taught some unbelieving Jews:

*He that heareth my word, and **believeth on him** that sent me, hath everlasting life, and shall not come into condemnation; but is passed from death unto life. John 5:24*

While Jesus was in Capernaum, some people asked Him

what works they should do to earn eternal life. He responded:

*This is the work of God, that ye **believe on him** whom he hath sent. John 6:29*

When a group of unbelieving Jews questioned Jesus on this subject, He proclaimed quite simply:

*He that **believeth on me** hath everlasting life.*
John 6:47

Jesus comforted a woman named Martha with these words:

*I am the resurrection, and the life: he that **believeth in me**, though he were dead, yet shall he live:*
John 11:25

While preaching to the Gentiles in Caesarea, the Apostle Peter said of Jesus:

*To him give all the prophets witness, that through his name whosoever **believeth in him** shall receive remission of sins. Acts 10:43*

In Acts 16, a terrified prison guard asked Paul and Silas, "what must I do to be saved?" They responded:

*"**Believe** on the Lord Jesus Christ, and thou shalt be saved, and thy house." Acts 16:30-31*

The Apostle Paul wrote to the believers in Rome:

*For I am not ashamed of the gospel of Christ: for it is the power of God unto salvation to every one that **believeth**... Romans 1:16*

While teaching in Capernaum, Jesus said:

*I am the bread of life: he that cometh to me shall never hunger; and he that **believeth on me** shall never thirst. John 6:35*

Jesus warned the Pharisees:

> ... *if ye* **believe not** *that I am he, ye shall die in your sins. John 8:24*

All I must do to reach heaven is believe in Jesus?

No, getting into heaven takes more than just saying, "I believe." First, you must understand the definition of the word "believe." According to *Strong's Concordance*, "believeth," as used in most of the verses just quoted, means "to entrust (espec. one's spiritual well-being to Christ): Commit (to trust), put in trust with."[1]

You see, Satan and all his demons believe Jesus Christ died for the sins of mankind. They believe He rose from the dead. They believe salvation is only available through faith in Him. But they are not saved because they refuse to put their trust in Him. To be saved, you must go beyond simply believing in Christ with your brain and be willing to trust in Him with your heart.

A daredevil was about to walk a tightrope across the Grand Canyon. One mistake would mean certain death on the jagged rocks below. With a huge crowd watching, an announcer asked how many people believed this fearless man could make it. Everyone roared with confidence.

Soon a chair was strapped on the daredevil's back. The man with the microphone asked, "Who believes he can make it with someone on his back?" Again, the entire crowd yelled with approval. After a moment the announcer asked, "Who is willing to get in the chair?" Dead silence.

1 *Strong's Exhaustive Concordance of the Bible,* Hendersonville, Tenn., Greek Dictionary of the New Testament pg. 58.

See the difference? It's one thing to say I believe he can make it, but quite another to put your complete trust in him.

It's the same way with salvation. To be truly saved takes more than just believing some facts. You must be willing to put your trust in Jesus Christ alone. How? By faith:

> *For ye are all the children of God **by faith in Christ Jesus.** Galatians 3:26*

> *Therefore being **justified by faith,** we have peace with God through our Lord Jesus Christ:*
> *Romans 5:1*

Salvation comes through faith, not good works:

> *Therefore we conclude that a man is **justified by faith** without the deeds of the law. Romans 3:28*

> *Wherefore the law was our schoolmaster to bring us unto Christ, that we might be **justified by faith**.*
> *Galatians 3:24*

Once you see that salvation comes through faith instead of works, it will be easier to understand that it is a free gift:

> *For by grace are ye saved through faith; and that not of yourselves: it is the **gift of God:** Not of works, lest any man should boast. Ephesians 2:8-9*

> *...the **gift of God** is eternal life through Jesus Christ our Lord. Romans 6:23*

God freely gives us eternal life. We don't earn it:

> *Being justified **freely** by his grace through the redemption that is in Christ Jesus. Romans 3:24*

> *And this is the record, that God hath **given to us eternal life,** and this life is in his Son. 1 John 5:10*

*Therefore as by the offence of one (Adam) judgment came upon all men to condemnation; even so by the righteousness of one (Jesus) the **free gift** came upon all men unto justification of life. Romans 5:18*

Don't I have to do any good works to get saved?

No. While it may seem logical that good works would be necessary for salvation, God's Word warns us not to be deceived by what seems right to us:

There is a way that seemeth right unto a man, but the end thereof are the ways of death. Proverbs 16:25

The truth is, good works will never save you:

"Not by works of righteousness which we have done, but according to his mercy he saved us…"

Titus 3:5

Knowing that a man is not justified by the works of the law, but by the faith of Jesus Christ… for by the works of the law shall no flesh be justified.

Galatians 2:16

Therefore by the deeds of the law there shall no flesh be justified in his sight… Romans 3:20

This crucial doctrine is repeated many times in Scripture:

*For by grace are ye saved through faith; and that not of yourselves: it is the gift of God: **Not of works,** lest any man should boast. Ephesians 2:8-9*

If good works could save, then Christ died for nothing:

I do not frustrate the grace of God: for if righteousness come by the law, then Christ is dead in vain. Galatians 2:21

If you attempt to earn heaven through your good works, you are really saying, "Jesus, I don't believe Your death was sufficient to pay for all my sins, so I will help pay the price with some of my own good deeds." ***How arrogant!***

Faith in Christ is the only way to heaven:

> *He that hath the Son hath life; and he that hath not the Son of God hath not life. 1 John 5:12*

Years ago, a slave auction was held along the banks of the Mississippi River. Everyone knew that a ruthless rich farmer was going to buy the biggest, strongest slave and work him tirelessly for the rest of his life.

However, a wealthy merchant who happened to be sailing down the river spotted the activities from his craft, and came ashore to watch. As the slave in question was brought to the block, a man in the back row explained to the merchant what was about to take place.

When the bidding began, the farmer yelled out a bid he thought could not be matched. But the merchant quickly topped the farmer's bid. The two bid back and forth, but soon the farmer reached his limit and left in defeat. The merchant approached the slave, gave him the keys to his chains and said, "You are free. I don't believe in slavery, I just didn't want him to own you."

Friend, that is what Jesus did for you and me. But instead of purchasing us with cash, He paid with His blood:

> *"What? Know ye not that your body is the temple of the Holy Ghost... and ye are not your own? **For ye are bought with a price...**" 1 Corinthians 6:19-20*

In the book of Acts, Paul says Christ purchased us *"**with his own blood"** (Acts 20:28).*

We were all born as slaves to sin. As a result, we deserve hell. But Jesus Christ died to pay the price for our sins. Because of His death and resurrection, we can be set free.

The slave had only to receive the keys to be set physically free. If we, by faith, receive God's gift of eternal life through Jesus Christ, we can be set spiritually free:

> *And ye shall know the truth, and the truth shall make you free. John 8:32*

Must my faith be in Christ alone?

Yes. A pastor traveled to a distant country, where people worship millions of gods. After preaching to a large group, he asked who would trust Jesus Christ as their Savior. Every hand went up. Knowing there was a problem, he clarified his message and repeated the question. Again, all hands shot skyward. Finally, he asked, "How many of you will trust Jesus Christ as your Savior and *reject* every other god?" Not one hand was raised.

You see, it's easy to simply add Jesus to a list of other people or things you are counting on for salvation. But to be truly born again requires faith in Jesus Christ alone, and a rejection of everything else.

Many people trust in Jesus *and* their good works... or in Jesus *and* their religion... or Jesus *and* their baptism, etc. But if you are trusting in anything in addition to Jesus, then you really aren't trusting Jesus at all.

Here's what happened to me

While in the military, a friend of mine invited me to church. My instant response was, "No thanks! I've had enough religion to last me a lifetime."

He knew I had been raised Catholic and wisely said, "Don't give up on God just because you gave up on the Catholic church."

A couple of friends of mine had already visited this church and returned with glowing reports, so I reluctantly agreed to join them.

The next Sunday morning, at least a thousand people jammed the church auditorium. After a few congregational songs, the pastor preached his sermon. He explained that Jesus Christ had come to earth and died on the cross to pay for our sins. He said that because of Christ's sacrifice, the gift of eternal life was available to anyone in the building.

Towards the end of the service, he asked those who wanted to trust Christ to come to the front. At that point, a noticeable pounding began to occur in my chest. I couldn't explain it. I just knew it was very weird... but very real.

As the pastor continued his invitation, the pounding increased. I could not shake the feeling I was supposed to walk up there. But I thought, "No way! Not in front of all these people."

Eventually, the singing stopped and just as quickly as the pounding began, it ended. I was stunned!

The pastor stepped back to the microphone and began to speak. Although I was sitting near the back row, I was convinced he was pointing his finger directly at me. And the words he spoke are permanently etched in my memory. "Many people have come forward and received Christ this morning, but I sense that someone here is still saying no to Jesus Christ."

I was sure he was talking directly to me. It was as if there was no one else in the auditorium. I was already sweating, but his following words nearly knocked me out:

"Whoever you are, I pray you don't die before you have another opportunity to trust Jesus Christ. If you do, you will burn forever in the lake of fire."

Talk about terrified! His words burned inside me, and I realized this wasn't just a man talking to me, it was God. I knew I was indeed headed for hell. I left the service in a cold sweat, with those words echoing in my ears.

Three days later, I attended another similar service. Once again, the pastor preached, and just as before, the pounding erupted in my chest. But this time, when the invitation began, I walked to the front.

I was met by a young man with a Bible, who explained God's plan of salvation, and asked me if I wanted to trust Christ. I did, and at that moment, I was born into God's family (Galatians 3:26). My name was recorded in the Lamb's Book of Life (Revelation 21:27). I had become a child of God (John 1:12).

What will you say to God?

Someday you and I will stand before God. When He asks us why He should allow us into heaven, there will be only two possible responses. One will be a works related approach, "You should let me in because I was a pretty good person. I didn't sin too much. I was fairly religious and I did the best I could." As you have already seen, this approach will not work.

The only other response will be, "You should let me into heaven because I trusted Jesus Christ as my Savior and His precious blood washed away all my sins:

"In hope of eternal life, which God, that cannot lie, promised before the world began." Titus 1:2

What does it mean to be born again?

One night Jesus told a religious leader named Nicodemus:

Except a man be born again, he cannot see the kingdom of God. Nicodemus saith unto him, How can a man be born when he is old? can he enter the second time into his mother's womb, and be born? Jesus answered, Verily, verily, I say unto thee, Except a man be born of water and of the Spirit, he cannot enter into the kingdom of God. That which is born of the flesh is flesh; and that which is born of the Spirit is spirit. Marvel not that I said unto thee, Ye must be born again. John 3:1-7

In this fascinating passage, we learn from Jesus Christ that to enter heaven, we must be "born again." Not understanding this, Nicodemus asked if one must crawl back into his mother's womb and be born a second time.

Jesus explained that coming out of our mother's womb was our physical birth. He calls this being born "of water" and "of the flesh." But to reach heaven, Jesus says we must be born a second time... spiritually.

This is a one-time act when you place your trust in Christ alone for your salvation and are born into God's family:

But as many as received him (Jesus), to them gave he power to become the sons of God, even to them that believe on his name: John 1:12

Notice, Jesus never said, "Except a man do good works, he cannot see the kingdom of God." He never said,

"Except a man keep the Ten Commandments, he cannot see the kingdom of God." Jesus said we must be "born again."

The Bible also refers to this event as being "saved." A prison guard asked Paul and Silas:

...Sirs, what must I do to be saved? And they said, Believe on the Lord Jesus Christ, and thou shalt be saved, and thy house. Acts 16:30-31

Acts 2:21 teaches the same thing:

And it shall come to pass, that whosoever shall call on the name of the Lord shall be saved.

Again, good works can't get you to heaven, but being saved will. So the spiritual battle rages. God wants you to be saved, while the devil doesn't.

So I must choose God or Satan, right?

Wrong! The Bible says:

*Wherefore as by the offence of one (Adam) judgment came upon all men to **condemnation**...*

Romans 5:18

Because of Adam's sin, you and I were born condemned sinners. Therefore, you don't have to choose the devil. He already owns you. You are his child, and on your way to hell. To do nothing is to remain his child.

*He that believeth on him (Jesus) is not condemned: but he that believeth not is **condemned already**, because he hath not believed in the name of the only begotten Son of God. John 3:18*

If you say, "I'll put it off and decide later," what you are really saying is, "I'll remain a lost hell-bound child of Satan and hope I live at least one more day."

You can become a Christian right now

Hopefully, God has convinced you of your need for Jesus Christ as your personal Savior. If so, you can be born again right now by simply asking God to save you:

For whosoever shall call upon the name of the Lord shall be saved. Romans 10:13

Pray to God in your own words. Talk to him like you would talk to a good friend. God is not impressed with stiff, formal prayers. He wants you to talk to Him from your heart. The key is believing in your heart what you say with your mouth:

That if thou shalt confess with thy mouth the Lord Jesus, and shalt believe in thine heart that God hath raised him from the dead, thou shalt be saved. For with the heart man believeth unto righteousness; and with the mouth confession is made unto salvation. Romans 10:9-10

Please don't put it off. Jesus is waiting for you:

Behold, I stand at the door, and knock: if any man hear my voice, and open the door, I will come in to him, and will sup with him, and he with me.

Revelation 3:20

If you would like to become a child of God, pray a prayer something like this from your heart:

Dear Jesus, I admit I am a sinner and I am sorry for all my sins. I realize my good works will never get me to heaven. I now see that the only way to heaven is through faith in You. Thank you for dying on the cross for me. Please forgive my sins and come into my heart and save me. Right now, I trust You alone for my salvation. In Jesus' name, Amen.

If you prayed a prayer like this and really meant it, you just made the most important decision of your life. You just became a brand new person:

*Therefore if any man be in Christ, he is a **new creature:** old things are passed away; behold, all things are become new. 2 Corinthians 5:17*

You are now a child of God. You received God's gift of eternal life and your name has been written in the Lamb's Book of Life in heaven. Angels in heaven are rejoicing over your salvation:

... there is joy in the presence of the angels of God over one sinner that repenteth. Luke 15:10

You now have an inheritance reserved in heaven for you (1 Peter 1:4) and you are a joint heir with Jesus Christ (Romans 8:17). A mansion is being built for you in heaven (John 14:2). Jesus Christ now lives in your heart (Ephesians 3:17) and the Holy Spirit will begin guiding you through your life (John 16:13). As you continue to grow as a Christian, you will learn much more about the miracle that just took place.

If you just trusted Christ, please flip over to page 60 and keep reading. You'll find some basic steps to will help you begin your new Christian life.

If you rejected Christ, you undoubtedly had a reason. Following are some of the most common reasons why people don't get saved. Please keep reading to see if yours appears.

Can't I wait until I'm older to trust Christ?

Of course you can, but you are ignoring one vital truth. There is no guarantee you will live to get older. In fact, you may not be here tomorrow. All you have is today. Every day, people die instantly in car wrecks, plane crashes, shootings, drownings, etc. How many of those people woke up on their fateful day, thinking, "I bet today is the day I'll get killed by a drunk driver." Nobody is guaranteed a tomorrow. That's why the Bible says:

...behold, now is the accepted time; behold, now is the day of salvation. 2 Corinthians 6:2

Plus, why would you want to wait? Why keep serving a cruel taskmaster like Satan when you can become a child of the King of kings, who wants to bless you?

What about all the Christian hypocrites?

Yes, there are hypocrites, but please don't let them keep you away from Christ. Someday we'll all stand before God:

And as it is appointed unto men once to die, but after this the judgment: Hebrews 9:27

When you die, you will answer for your life and the hypocrite will answer for his. Picture this. You have just died. You are ushered into God's presence for judgment. As you stand trembling before His throne, God's booming voice rings out, "Did you trust My Son as your Savior?"

Are you really going to want to say, "No, God, I rejected your Son and the gift of eternal life because there was this hypocrite who lived across the street from me?"

No, on that day, you'll know you should have trusted Christ. But it will be too late.

If I become a Christian, won't it ruin all my fun?

It all depends upon your definition of the word "fun." If you mean, "Will I have to give up my sin?," then you need to understand the truth about sin. While sin does often provide a short term thrill, in the end, its price is always much too high.

Dave had a loving wife, three small children and a great job. But he wanted to have some "fun." For over a year he did, with a secretary at his office. One night, after a visit to his doctor, he was forced to come home and confess to his wife his unfaithfulness. She began screaming in anger, but he stopped her, saying, "Wait... it gets much worse."

"I just learned I have AIDS. I will probably die... and so will you. Our three children will probably be orphans." Dave now knew the price for his "fun." He also learned why the Bible said:

...the way of transgressors is hard. Proverbs 13:15

For several years, a high-flying executive had great "fun" at bars. Alcohol was his main entertainment. But when he was killed after slamming into a semi on a freeway after downing a few too many drinks, he learned the price for his "fun" was more than he wanted to pay. But it was too late.

Drugs were Jason's "fun" until some bad LSD fried his brain. He lost touch with reality and is now a vegetable. If he had his mind, he'd know his "fun" cost far more than he ever imagined.

You may be enjoying your sin now, but remember, payment day is coming. And you won't like the price.

So will becoming a Christian ruin all your fun? No, that

is a lie from the devil. The truth is, until you become a Christian, you don't know what real fun is.

Isn't Christianity just for the weak?

Many skeptics contend Christianity is a crutch for people who are too weak-minded to think for themselves. In reality, the opposite is true. Those who put forth the mental effort to search for truth usually become Christians. Those who use the cop-out "Christianity is only for the weak" are in reality the weak ones... too weak or lazy to do their own thinking. With eternity in heaven or hell at stake, don't be a fool by allowing somebody else to do your thinking for you.

I don't have time for God. I want to make money.

Picture this. You just died. Angels escort you before God's throne. You fall on your face in awe, and God asks, "Did you trust My Son as your Lord and Savior?

Can you imagine yourself blurting out, "Well, no, God, but I did run a very successful business and my gross annual income did triple over a ten year period."

Your financial bracket will be of no importance when you stand before God. On that day, you will wish you had memorized:

> *For what shall it profit a man, if he shall gain the whole world, and lose his own soul? Mark 8:36*

Luke 12 records the story of a man who ignored Christ so he could make money. God said to him:

> *Thou fool, this night thy soul shall be required of thee: then whose shall those things be, which thou hast provided? Luke 12:20*

All your earthly possessions will mean nothing when you stand before God. Two men stood at the funeral of a wealthy friend. One whispered, "Did you hear how much Hank left behind?" The other replied, "Yeah, all of it."

For we brought nothing into this world, and it is certain we can carry nothing out. 1 Timothy 6:7

After you die, you'll know your relationship with Jesus Christ was far more important than making money. If you are smart, you won't wait until it's too late.

I could never love God after what He did to me

Many people are bitter against God because of a past tragedy. You need to know that Satan may be using your tragedy to doom you to hell. The devil may be constantly bringing the tragedy to your mind to harden your heart against God. He may be keeping the bitterness fresh in your mind because as long as you remain bitter against God, you will never be saved.

Please don't let the devil use your tragedy to doom you to hell. Understand that Satan, not God, is your enemy. Satan is a destroyer (John 10:10), but God is love (1 John 4:16). God loves you and wants to save you so He can begin healing your heart.

Imagine a man falling into a life of crime. Though his mother hates what he does, she continues to love her son. One day he murders a police officer, is convicted, and sentenced to death. When execution day arrives, the convict hears the dreaded footsteps approaching his cell. His door swings open, but instead of turning left, towards the death chamber, they turn right. In amazement, the convicted killer is escorted to the front exit, and set free.

"What's going on?" he asks.

"The death penalty has been paid," a guard tells him.

"Last night, your mother was executed in your place. She willingly died for you, so you could go free."

That's what Jesus did for you. You deserved the eternal execution chamber, but God sent Jesus Christ to die in your place so you could go free. Don't remain bitter against God. Become a Christian right now so God can begin changing your heart and life.

If Christianity is right, why are there so few Christians?

Most people reject Christ because their father, Satan has blinded their mind:

> *In whom the god of this world (Satan) hath blinded the minds of them which believe not, lest the light of the glorious gospel of Christ, who is the image of God, should shine unto them. 2 Corinthians 4:4*

Know it or not, you are in a spiritual war. And you have a powerful spiritual enemy who wants to destroy you:

> *The thief (Satan) cometh not, but for to steal, and to kill, and to destroy... John 10:10*

John Newton referred to this spiritual blindness in his classic Christian hymn, *Amazing Grace,* "I once was lost, but now am found, *Was blind, but now I see.*"

Are you spiritually blind?

Here's how you can tell. You have two options: trust Jesus Christ by faith and receive the gift of eternal life, or reject Him and burn forever in hell's flames. If you choose the latter, you are spiritually blind. You are under Satan's power and living according to his desires:

> *Wherein in time past ye walked according to the course of this world, **according to the prince of the power of the air (Satan),** the spirit that now worketh in the children of disobedience: Ephesians 2:2*

God sent the Apostle Paul to preach to the Gentiles...

> *To open their eyes, and to turn them from darkness to light, and from **the power of Satan** unto God, that they may receive forgiveness of sins, and inheritance among them which are sanctified by faith that is in me. Acts 26:18*

My prayer is that your eyes will be opened and you will be turned from the power of Satan to God through faith in Jesus Christ. To stop you from being saved, Satan will try to remove from your mind the words of this book:

> *Those by the way side are they that hear; then cometh the devil, and taketh away the word out of their hearts, **lest they should believe and be saved.***
> *Luke 8:12*

Please ask God to remove the spiritual blindness so you can see your lost and deceived state. You can still ask Jesus to save you. God wants you to trust Him. Jesus said:

> *...him that cometh to me I will in no wise cast out.*
> *John 6:37*

Isn't your position intolerant?

Many lost religious people consider this message intolerant of other religions. Some even call it "hateful." You decide. Picture this hypothetical scenario...

A doctor has extensive experience with a particular illness. He knows if a certain medication is prescribed, the patient will die. At a conference, he hears three doctors say they are about to prescribe this medication for patients with this particular illness.

What should he do?

Should the risk of offending other doctors cause him to remain silent? Should the risk of being labeled "intolerant" stop him from speaking up? Of course not. He must speak up, regardless of the consequences, and attempt to save those lives.

So it is with this book. Sharing with you these truths from God's Word is neither intolerant nor hateful. You must be warned that heaven or hell await. Wanting you to go to heaven is not intolerant, it's love. If you happen to belong to a religion that is leading you to hell, love demands you be warned.

Why don't you let people decide for themselves?

Suppose while hiking up a mountain you saw a blind man about to step off a cliff to certain death hundreds of feet below. Would you let him decide for himself? No, you would run to him and grab him. You would do everything possible to stop him.

Without Christ in your life, you are spiritually blind. You don't see that you are approaching a cliff leading to eternal damnation. If someone gave you this book, it's because they care about you. They know you don't see what's ahead, so they, out of concern for your soul, feel compelled to warn you, like you would do for a physically blind man.

What if you are wrong about all this?

You can gamble that I am wrong, but are you willing to risk it? Imagine this scenario: A gambler loses all his money in Las Vegas. The casino offers one last wager...

"If you win, you get all your money back. If we win, then two of our security men will haul you down to the basement and toss you into our huge roaring furnace."

Obviously, nobody in their right mind would risk those consequences. Yet, this is the gamble you take every day you reject Christ. If you die, you are guaranteed an eternity in the flames of hell.

This is not a scare tactic, but a heart-felt warning. When a mother tells her child, "Don't touch the stove," is she only trying to scare him? No. She warns him because she loves him and does not want him to suffer. Many children ignore this warning and only learn the truth after their flesh begins to sizzle... but then it's too late.

After death, it will be too late to change your mind. Your eternal destiny will be set. The prophet Isaiah asked this all-important question:

Who among us shall dwell with the devouring fire? who among us shall dwell with everlasting burnings? Isaiah 33:14

There is only one way to escape the eternal flames of hell. Will you accept it?

How shall we escape, if we neglect so great salvation... Hebrews 2:3

Will you repent of your sins and trust Christ as your Savior? You have everything to gain, and nothing to lose. God wants to save you right now:

For this is good and acceptable in the sight of God our Savior: **Who will have all men to be saved...**
1 Timothy 2:3-4

If you continue to reject Christ as your Savior, the rest of this book will be of no help to you.

But be warned one final time, no matter what your excuse, if you die without Christ, hell will be your eternal home.

Please make Jesus Christ your Savior right now, before it is eternally too late.

What should I do now that I'm a Christian?

If you just made Jesus Christ your Savior, you are now a baby Christian. And like a newborn physical baby, you need to begin growing. Here are a few basic steps to help you get started in your new Christian life.

Join a good Bible preaching church

God's Word gives us this command:

Not forsaking the assembling of ourselves together, as the manner of some is; but exhorting one another: and so much the more, as ye see the day approaching. Hebrews 10:25

Ask God to lead you to the church He wants you to attend. Through a local church you will meet and fellowship with other believers. Plus, hearing God's Word preached and taught will help you grow. The church will also provide a place where you can serve God, which will further aid your spiritual growth.

Get baptized

As a new Christian, you should follow Christ's example and be baptized. Biblical baptism is the immersion of a new believer under water. Throughout the New Testament, right after trusting in Christ, new believers were baptized:

Then they that gladly received his word were baptized... Acts 2:41

In Acts 8:36-37, the Ethiopian eunuch said:

*See, here is water; what doth hinder ꞓ.ꞓ to be baptized? And Philip said, **If thou believest with all thine heart, thou mayest.***

Because you must believe in Christ before being baptized, infant baptisms don't count. Since infants cannot believe in Christ, they cannot be scripturally baptized. So if you were baptized as an infant and just now got saved, you need to be baptized again.

Read your Bible every day

The Bible is God's love letter to you. Each time you read it, you will grow spiritually (1 Peter 2:2) and get to know God a little better. Reading God's Word will solidify your beliefs, and equip you to defend them:

Study to shew thyself approved unto God, a workman that needeth not to be ashamed, rightly dividing the word of truth. 2 Timothy 2:15

Among other things, reading the Bible will cleanse your life (Psalm 119:9), keep you from sin (Psalm 119:11), increase your faith (Romans 10:17), and be your guide:

Thy word is a lamp unto my feet, and a light unto my path. Psalm 119:105

Pray

Now that you are a Christian, you can talk directly to God through prayer. God gives us this instruction:

Call unto me, and I will answer thee, and shew thee great and mighty things, which thou knowest not. Jeremiah 33:3

Biblical prayer is not reciting cold, stiff, pre-written words:

But when ye pray, use not vain repetitions, as the heathen do: for they think that they shall be heard for their much speaking. Matthew 6:7

True prayer is sharing your heart with God:

*Trust in him at all times; ye people, **pour out your heart before him**... Psalm 62:8*

God's Word tells us to pray about everything, including our needs (Matthew 6:11) and desires (Philippians 4:6). We should pray for each other (James 5:16), for our enemies (Luke 6:28), for the sick (James 5:14-16), and for wisdom (James 1:5).

We should also regularly thank God for his goodness (Psalm 100:4). Best of all, we can pray anytime:

The Lord is nigh unto all them that call upon him, to all that call upon him in truth. Psalm 145:18

Tell others what Jesus has done for you

As a Christian, you will want to share with others what Jesus has done for you. Nothing is more important or rewarding than telling people about Christ:

Let him know, that he which converteth the sinner from the error of his way shall save a soul from death, and shall hide a multitude of sins. James 5:20

There is no better way for you to invest your time:

The fruit of the righteous is a tree of life; and he that winneth souls is wise. Proverbs 11:30

Conclusion

The purpose of this book was to show you from the one and only authoritative source what awaits you after death, and to help you settle your eternal destiny. I pray that after reading this book, you have trusted Jesus Christ as your own personal Savior.

If you have, I would love to hear about it. You can e-mail me at:

rjones@chick.com

Or write me at:
Rick Jones
c/o Chick Publications
PO Box 3500
Ontario, CA 91761

God bless you.

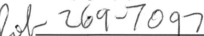